# No Biography

## Parts of a Life
## in Tanka

Alan Hill

HappenStance

ISBN 978-1-905939-58-9

Sequence series, 3

**Previous publications:**
*The Green Tide*, Rivelin Press, 1975
*To Rocamadour*, Redbeck Press, 2005 (in which some of the tanka in this volume first appeared)

Printed by The Dolphin Press
www.dolphinpress.co.uk

Published in 2010 by Happen*Stance*
21 Hatton Green, Glenrothes, Fife KY7 4SD
nell@happenstancepress.com
www.happenstancepress.com

**Orders:**
Individual pamphlets £4.00 (includes UK P&P).
Please make cheques payable to Happen*Stance* or order through PayPal in the website shop.

*for my family*

Aged nine, on a bus,
watching strangers passing by.
Then a thought, that I
too, glimpsed by those in the street,
was a stranger passing by.

It's strange. She's not tall
and her hair is dark, not fair—
not my type at all.
Yet, why I cannot tell,
at our first meeting, I fell

Su Shi was banished
into a remote province
where he lived and died
obscure. Too poor to travel,
he received the wild geese.

Loving the whole of
creation is difficult.
Yes, the spirochaete
of syphilis calls for the
most determined devotion.

To please his friends, O
made himself into a drum,
silent until struck.
Thus he was not heard until
the army's march had begun.

*(At Silverton)*
The patter of rain
and the lick of the fire;
the cat flicks an ear;
the slowing globe spins time, which
passes quietly here.

I came to Scotland
and lost my way. But—praise the
gods of mist and peat—
I discovered whisky, and
at length, found a narrow path.

Sunday. My birthday.
Forty-four. Nothing special.
Went walking alone.
Noted the sunshine, but thought
a good deal about money.

The west wind blows cold;
the garden bees are silent;
the swifts are long gone.
But chimneys and tree-tops are
burnished gold in the late sun.

Deliver us from
the hard eyes and set jaws of
the will to power;
and from those who confuse God
with their own identities.

Sleepless, at dawn I
watch the snow-reflected light.
Only she is warm.
I touch her sleeping form, but
still she sleeps. I am alone.

Irises flutter,
seem almost to blink against
the wind and the sun;
so elaborately shaped
and so delicately strong.

I am a small cog
employed by the Big Wheel.
When he moves slightly
I must spin round I know not
how many wearying turns.

A pebble, that shone
like a jewel when it lay
in its clear pool—
out of water, in plain day,
has dulled into these flat words.

At fifty, sometimes
I forget my age. It seems
that I could run and
vault a five-barred gate with ease;
but my right knee disagrees.

Waiting for the voice
that will tell me what to say.
But only silence,
like an empty street at night,
with footsteps walking away.

Last October, my
father planted wallflowers.
Now, in coloured ranks,
they're ready for inspection,
as if he were still alive.

The advancing dark,
like a progressive disease,
lingers more each day;
grows bolder with each attack,
and goes more slowly away.

After April rain
reluctant blossoms obey
the indifferent sun
which blundered out today when
spring came, and Kate went away.

*(Near Armagh)*
With a heavy stick
I killed a myxy rabbit.
Three blows only broke
its back; the fourth its neck, and
my taste for intervention.

Drifting clouds' shadows
darken but do not disturb
these quiet hill slopes,
so quiet you can almost
hear the slow Earth turning.

Snow falls gently on
daffodils in the garden,
white flakes vying with
the petals of the cherry
in their quickness of dying.

*Do not go gentle,*
he said, *into that good night* . . .
too young to know the
weariness of survival
long after losing the fight.

*(At Fownhope)*
After heavy rain,
a thrush sings in the orchard;
white violets and
celandines in the steep lane;
and sunlight on the far wood.

*(In Hospital 1)*
Naked, and with all
superficialities
reduced to bare life,
as I was born, rolled now to
the adjudicating knife.

*(In Hospital 2)*
The perfect crimson
ball of the rising sun burns
through the east window.
After a sleepless night, oh
what relief that the Earth turns.

I am the Ice King,
impassive and *comme il faut.*
When you weep like a
distressed child, my snow heart melts
but my frozen arms can't move.

Short of mental breath,
I sing no swelling themes, but
write my five-line stints
like chipped-off flakes of paint that
disclose the dry grain beneath.

Farting poems, my
flatulent muse produces
airy nothings that
give me a sweet relief but,
alas, embarrass my friends.

See me, the teacher,
like a railway porter,
guiding travellers
to destinations which I
know only from the posters.

Something is wrong. My
barber knows my name, recalls
what I recall—but
as he cuts, the hair that falls
is white, not like mine at all.

Are teachers consoled
that the distance by which their
students outstrip them
is perhaps the best measure
of professional success?

*You are not,* she said,
*the kind of man girls sleep with.*
*No!* she said, *You are*
*the kind they want to marry.*
This news did not rejoice him.

November! I like
these dark melancholy days.
This is my month, for
in the dark and dying year,
I took my first breath of life.

I made a contract
with the future, as I thought;
but it did not last.
The fault was not the future's;
I'd confused it with the past.

This head is a house,
gardens trim, paintwork gleaming.
The windows, though, are
barred and secret; and inside
could that be someone screaming?

The dying sun glows
moodily among dark clouds.
Behind the bare trees,
deep tracks lead across the snow,
marking the way we must go.

I knew the painter.
I knew that boathouse, and those
deep blue shadows, their
flickering caught in paint. And
I knew the girl he took there.

That quiet cloister,
the grey lake lapping the shore,
those wild flowers—
the story I did not write
that summer in Vadstena.

Even the falling
winter call of a starling
reminds me of home,
and the apple trees that I
haven't seen for forty years.

Small white butterflies
flap and flutter up and down.
How far you have flown,
little white butterflies, all
the way from my childhood days.

At Aston Cantlow
there's a turn to the village
by a broad greensward
where fear betrayed me once,
almost sixty years ago.

Another Christmas—
the card to his widow for
the twenty-third year;
and sometimes, still, his silence
is all that I can hear.

Suppose Charles Darwin
had not been a gentleman.
He would have needed
to earn his living. All the
churches might still have been full.

If men were thought of
as musical instruments,
Billy Connolly
would always come to my mind
as a Glaswegian trombone.

Quiet autumn days.
I seem now mostly to be
made of memories,
like old wounds, sometimes aching
according to the weather.

That is a strange day
when you wake to discover
age has drifted down
imperceptibly, like dust,
and you're totally covered.

The birds feel it.
They are calling more, and all
their songs are changing.
It's in the light, in the air,
stir, excitement, everywhere.

At seventy-five
I'm more aware, more alive
to change—in the air,
on the ground, and in the way
the light grows stronger every day.

No biography.
Just small fragments and murmurs
breaking the surface,
like the tiny island peaks
of dim, submarine mountains.

I keep losing words.
They disappear between
brain and tongue, like coins
that fall and roll out of sight,
hiding for days. Even weeks.

I talk to the dead
continually—old friends,
colleagues, relations.
They smile a lot, nod, and
sometimes we laugh together.

It's not surprising
that we find philosophy
somewhat confusing.
Its critiques are often right;
its solutions always wrong.

A blackbird woke me,
singing before this March dawn,
ringing his alarm,
warning all of us that it's
spring, and the garden is his.

*Is it true?* she asked,
*just as you wrote it—all the*
*sorrow and glory?*
Smiling, he said, *Truth lies in*
*the poem, not the story.*

We must all follow
the inescapable path
of the labyrinth,
into its empty centre
where nothing is but oneself.